Original title:
Tide of the Soul

Copyright © 2025 Creative Arts Management OÜ
All rights reserved.

Author: Samuel Kensington
ISBN HARDBACK: 978-1-80587-360-0
ISBN PAPERBACK: 978-1-80587-830-8

## Waves of Whispers

The ocean shouts, but only I hear,
A fish does a dance, oh dear, oh dear.
Seagulls gossip, squawking and screech,
While crabs make cocktails, on the beach.

Sandcastles crumble, kings take a fall,
With buckets and spades, we give it our all.
A tidal wave of laughter rolls in,
As the waves play tag with our silly sin.

## Currents of the Heart

In the whirlpool of love, I slip and I slide,
Hearts doing somersaults, like a wacky ride.
The jellyfish float, with grace oh so odd,
While starfish give winks, like a cosmic nod.

My heart, a small boat, on a sea of romance,
Caught in the currents, I leap in my pants.
But sharks dressed in suits try to steal my fun,
I paddle away laughing, oh, what have I done?

**The Sea Within**

Deep in my belly, the waves start to churn,
A tickle of laughter, oh how I yearn.
A clam with a pearl that thinks it's a star,
While seaweed giggles, it's all bizarre.

Octopus poets write verses of woe,
While hermit crabs boast, 'Look at my glow!'
Bubbles of joy burst, as friendships arise,
In the sea of my spirit, there's no need for ties.

**Echoes Beneath the Surface**

Echoes of laughter ripple through time,
With dolphins in tuxedos, they dance in a line.
All the fish join in with a splish and a splash,
A party beneath, oh what a bash!

Whispers of wisdom from a wise old whale,
Tell tales of a sea where the goblins sail.
With mermaids who giggle and sing silly songs,
Our hearts grow lighter, where laughter belongs.

## Waves of Unspoken Truths

Beneath the surface, giggles flow,
Promises tangled, a comedic show.
Whispers crash like playful splashes,
Secrets dance where the shoreline dashes.

Mismatched socks on a sunny spree,
The ocean's sarcasm is quite the fee.
Salty laughter on a windy day,
Truths ride waves, then bounce away.

## The Abyss of Longing Hearts

In the deep where desires swim,
Clumsy fish flounder, on a whim.
Heartbeats echo like a silly tune,
Lost in love's underwater commune.

Seaweed tangled, it's quite bizarre,
A soggy note floats from afar.
Wishful winks from crabs on the sand,
They pinch at fate, it's all unplanned.

## **Glistening Traces of Memory**

Footprints left on a sandy shore,
Tell tales of laughter, who could ask for more?
Shells whisper stories of days gone bright,
A starfish chuckles at the fading light.

Each glimmer hides a silly surprise,
Like jellybeans tossed from hideous pies.
Memories skip like stones on the sea,
Bouncing back, they laugh with glee.

## Wandering Visions on the Beach

Seagulls cackle, they've lost the plot,
Chasing dreams like they're good as caught.
Waves draw doodles on the frothy crest,
A mermaid grins, she's quite the jest.

Sandy sandwiches float by like clouds,
While beach balls bounce, causing proud crowds.
In this circus of sun and fun,
Laughter ebbs with the setting sun.

## Liquid Echoes of Tomorrow

In puddles left from rain's embrace,
The reflections dance with silly grace.
Tomorrow's laughter splashes wide,
A jellyfish in a tuxedo, filled with pride.

With bubbles bouncing off my toes,
The future sloshes where nobody goes.
A rubber duck spins in delight,
As I chase waves of hopes so bright.

## Journey through Untamed Waters

I sailed my cereal in a bowl,
A pirate ship on a breakfast roll.
With marshmallow cannons, we took the chance,
To conquer the milk in a crunchy dance.

A dolphin laughs from my spoon's tip,
While I bravely embark on this flaky trip.
The ocean of oats swirls all around,
In the wild waters, joy's the sound.

## The Rhythm of Ebbing Light

The sun dips low, a disco ball,
It spins and sways, oh what a thrall!
With shadows twisting on the sand,
A conga line of seagulls, isn't it grand?

Each wave a wink, each splash a tease,
As crabs boogie with the breeze.
Under the beach umbrella's sway,
We dance with light that's on display.

## **Enchantment of Water's Veil**

A waterfall of socks, lost in a whirl,
Twisting and twirling, a laundry world.
Each sock a fish in a washing sea,
Dancing around, oh look at me!

With bubbles popping like tiny stars,
The soapsuds travel near and far.
In this enchanted rinse and spin,
Laughter bubbles from within.

## The Flowing Essence

In a river of dreams, we all drift along,
Riding waves made of giggles, floating on a song.
Paddling with spoons and bursting with cheer,
The water is bubbly, bringing smiles near.

Splashing goldfish, they dance with flair,
Swimming in circles, with nary a care.
We giggle as we float on our inflatable swan,
Life is a circus, from dusk until dawn.

## Depths of Longing

Beneath the surface, funny fish say,
"We had a great party, but where's the buffet?"
With jellybeans sparkling, they throw a feast,
But they can't find the chips, oh what a beast!

A penguin named Phil lost his way on a spree,
He dove down for treasure, but it's all sea debris.
He gave a loud chuckle, with a comical pout,
"Who knew that the ocean was all about clout?"

## Ebb and Flow of Emotion

Like a seesaw of laughter, we rise and we fall,
Sometimes I'm giggling, and sometimes I brawl.
With a rubber ducky bobbing beside me,
It quacks out my woes, as silly as can be.

A wave of confusion as my socks disappear,
Washed up on the shore—now that's quite the fear!
Yet I wade through the laughter, feeling so whole,
Riding the currents that tickle my soul.

## **Whirlpools of Reflection**

In a whirlpool of humor, I spin and I sway,
Chasing my thoughts, as they drift far away.
Two clowns on a tightrope, balancing with flair,
Juggling their worries, they float through the air.

A parrot that squawks, "Is it dinner or snack?"
With his beak in the chips, he won't cut me slack.
Yet amidst all this laughter, my heart feels so light,
As I spiral through giggles, all day and all night.

## The Calm Before Awakening

The snooze button's hit, oh what a mess,
Dreams of breakfast, but I must confess,
Pajamas still on as I roam the floor,
Coffee's a friend, but I'm wanting more.

The sun peeks through, a cheeky surprise,
Waking my spirit in bright, sunny skies.
With a yawn and a stretch, I finally rise,
Ready to dance like a pair of spies.

## Ebb and Flow of Spirit

Like waves on the shore, my laughter does sway,
One minute I'm serious, then I'm at play.
Tickle my funny bone, watch me retreat,
Jumping around like a fish on a seat.

In and out of quirks, I'm lost and I'm found,
Life's perfect dance, with a silly sound.
Bouncing on whims, never quite dull,
With every good chuckle, I always feel full.

## Requiem of the Restless Waves

Oh restless waves, with a flair for the tease,
You splash and you crash, aiming only to please.
Whispers of laughter, with each little swirl,
As seaweed does bob, in a dance that does twirl.

The crabs do a jig, while the seagulls applaud,
Ignoring the sun, feeling slightly odd.
The ocean's our stage, with antics galore,
In this tribute to fun, who could ask for more?

## Reflections in the Ocean's Eye

In the ocean's mirror, a funny sight waits,
With splashes and giggles from sea's playful mates.
Who knew a reflection could make one chuckle?
With every wave breaking, I just want to snuggle.

Bubbles arise, like giggles in bloom,
Each ripple a joke, filling up the room.
The sea's a comedian, with tales to unfold,
In each subtle wave, new adventures are told.

## **Driftwood Dreams**

A stick floats by, with tales to tell,
It dreams of seas and sandy shell.
Each wave a laugh, a giggle, a roar,
As it bounces on shores, forevermore.

It wears a hat made of seaweed green,
A fashion choice that's rarely seen.
A seagull laughs as it steals the show,
While the sun sets on the driftwood glow.

## Deep Currents of Reflection

In the depths, fish chat about the day,
While turtles joke and mermaids sway.
A crab complains of his right-side pinch,
Saying, 'This shell's just one big clinch!'

The octopus paints with swirling ink,
His masterpiece makes everyone think.
You might not see it at first glance,
But the ocean's a party, come join the dance!

## Serenade of the Seawind

The wind whispers secrets to the shore,
Tickling the trees, asking for more.
A sandcastle king wears a crown made of clay,
And he sways with the breeze in a quirky way.

A starfish croons with a twinkling smile,
While sea foam giggles, dancing a while.
The ocean sings with a bubbly cheer,
Even the barnacles join in near!

## Waves of Forgotten Longing

Once a fish swam with dreams to explore,
But swapped his fins for a beach ball score.
He lounges in sun, with shades on his face,
"Who needs the ocean? I've found my place!"

Old shells whisper tales of days gone past,
Of mermaids and pirates, oh how they'd last.
Yet now they sit quietly, reminiscing,
Just wishing for waves, that they're still missing.

**Drift into Distant Shores**

Sailing on a noodle boat, quite absurd,
Chasing after jellyfish, so deferred.
A surfboard shaped like toast, what a sight,
Splashing with a crab, oh, what delight!

A seagull stole my sandwich, what a flap,
I chased it down, it took a funny nap.
On sun-kissed sands, I danced on my toes,
While beach balls bounced, where no one knows.

The ocean whispered jokes, oh so sly,
As I slipped on seaweed, went for a fly.
Fish made faces, tickling my feet,
In the laughter of waves, life feels so sweet!

And as the sun sets, so bright and bold,
I gather all the memories, bite-sized and gold.
For all the quirks that life has to send,
I drift into dreams, where silliness blends.

## The Heart's Navigational Chart

With a compass made of candy, I steer,
Guided by giggles and waves of cheer.
Maps filled with doodles, drawn by my cat,
Paw prints on parchment – oh, imagine that!

Charts that lead to a fountain of soda,
Mermaids throwing parties – what a moda!
Round about the corners where crabs wear ties,
And jellybeans float under purple skies.

I plotted a course for the land of fun,
Where laughter beams brighter than the sun.
Asteroids made of chocolate are fierce,
In this world of whimsy, my heart can pierce.

Navigating through hiccups and laughs galore,
The waves crash softly, begging for more.
With each twist and turn, I truly find,
The map of my heart is silly, yet kind.

## **Resilience in the Ripples**

Wobbly waves make me giggle and sway,
As I stumble through puddles in zestful play.
Rubber ducks quack, cheering me on,
In this bouncy world, my worries are gone.

A surfer with a tutu, what a sight,
Riding the big swells, oh, what a fright!
Fish in bowties swim past with ease,
While I collapse laughing, just like the breeze.

But through the ripples, I gather my might,
Each splash a reminder, oh, what a flight!
Facing faceplants and silly falls low,
With each little wave, my spirit can grow.

So bring on the foamy, the fun, the laugh!
In this ocean of quirks, I'll carve my path.
For every droplet can amass with grace,
Into a ripple of joy, a bright, shining space.

## **Heartstrings by the Water's Edge**

By the water's edge, I strum a fish tune,
As dolphins sway gently, under the moon.
Octopuses dance, their limbs in a flurry,
While squirrels apply sunscreen in a hurry.

Heartstrings made of jelly, so sweet and light,
Tugged by the breeze, they wiggle just right.
A marshmallow boat drifts in a floaty race,
And laughter bubbles up, a gleeful embrace.

Seagulls join in, squawking their cheer,
As I sing to the tide, for all to hear.
With each little wave, my spirit sings loud,
In this joyful mess, I'm eternally proud.

So let's cheer for the quirks, the giggles, the sighs,
For heartstrings by water are the grandest highs.
In the symphony of silliness, I'll forever dwell,
The laughter of life, oh, how it compels!

## Driftwood Dreams

Wooden dreams float by, quite absurd,
They dance with the waves, not a single word.
A crab joins in, with moves so slick,
While seagulls laugh, they play their trick.

The ocean whispers, 'Come take a ride!'
With driftwood hats, let's all collide.
We'll surf on laughter, and splash with glee,
As jellyfish giggle, oh can't you see?

Oysters wear pearls, all grumpy and shy,
While barnacles sing a cheerful lullaby.
A clumsy old starfish trips on his leg,
Saying, 'Who needs shoes? I'm truly a keg!'

So let's chase the sun, or maybe the moon,
With surfboard dreams, oh let's make it soon.
For joy is the current that sweeps us away,
In driftwood adventures, we'll frolic and sway.

## The Currents Within

In belly buttons lie currents unseen,
Wiggling and jiggling, a silly routine.
They swirl and they giggle like fish on a spree,
Oh, what a ruckus, come join in with me!

The more that we wiggle, the more that we laugh,
Like dolphins at play, we just cannot chaff!
A shoal of good vibes swims up to the shore,
Tickling our toes, always wanting some more.

Not all currents are serious, some just want fun,
Like currents of laughter beneath the hot sun.
Catch a wave of humor, it's silly and bright,
With waves rolling in, let's dance through the night!

So ride on the currents that tickle your soul,
For giggles and chuckles are surely the goal.
With smiles and high-fives, we chart out our course,
In the ocean of laughter, we're spreading the force!

## Whispers of the Moonlit Shore

The moon spills secrets on the dark sea,
Whispers of laughter, come join in with me.
A crab in a tux, he waltzes with style,
As clams make a fuss, they giggle the while.

Shells tell tall tales, as tides flip and flop,
With stories of mermaids who can't seem to stop.
They're knitting up sweaters for fish in a trance,
While turtles play tag, oh let's take a chance!

A starfish declared it a fancy dress night,
With glittery seashells, it's quite a sight.
The jellyfish glow with their lights all aglow,
And dance at moon's rhythm, to put on a show.

So stroll down the shore, let the moonbeam unfold,
Embrace all the joy that the night has to hold.
The whispers of merriment carry on the breeze,
With laughter and joy, let's dance with such ease!

## Embrace of the Ocean's Heart

From the heart of the sea, a tickle of cheer,
With manta rays flying, they sing loud and clear.
A whale in a bowtie spins round for a laugh,
While fish throw confetti, now there's a party half!

Crabs in a conga, they dance on the sand,
With laughter like bubbles, they stick to the plan.
The tides pull them close, a slippery band,
As seaweed joins in, wiggling on hand.

An octopus juggles the pearls on his head,
While gulls look on with a chuckle instead.
The sea otters giggle, as they float in delight,
Wrapping up friendships, they hug through the night.

So ride on the laughter that flows from the sea,
Where jests and pinches blend perfectly.
In the embrace of joy, we'll swim 'til we drop,
With the ocean's soft heartbeat, let laughter not stop!

## Beneath the Glistening Skies

Under the sun, we find our fun,
Seagulls squawk, their antics spun.
Drinks in hand, we laugh away,
While crabs do the cha-cha by the bay.

Sunburned noses shine so bright,
Chasing waves, what a silly sight!
Flip-flops flying, shoes in tow,
Oh, the places our feet will go!

Buckets for castles, not for sand,
With every splash, we form a band.
Sandwiches fly, a seagull dash,
Picnic chaos, what a splash!

Joy in the chaos, laughter reigns,
Beneath the skies, no room for pains.
With quirks and gags, our hearts we free,
Dancing to waves, just you and me.

## Horizons of Hope

Balancing dreams on a surfboard's edge,
With a goofy grin, I make my pledge.
To ride the waves of life so bright,
And laugh with joy through day and night.

Paddle out where the wild winds blow,
Finding peace in the ebb and flow.
Tangled hair, a surfer's crown,
While waves of laughter never drown.

Fish tales tall, we spin and weave,
As dolphins dance, we can't believe.
Each splash a chance to ride the highs,
Living dreams beneath vast skies.

With every wave, a giggle grows,
In salty air, my spirit glows.
Horizons beckon, what a thrill,
Seizing moments, chasing joy at will.

## Surrender to the Sea's Embrace

Waves whisper secrets, oh, what a tease,
Bobbing along, as light as a breeze.
Dancing in foam, my worries shed,
In the embrace, I'm happily led.

Floaties and laughter tie us in knots,
With sunscreen globs, we take our shots.
Sandy snacks and sandy toes,
Wild ocean tales, well, nobody knows!

A crab with sass, he steals my fries,
While turtles wink with knowing eyes.
Under the sun, we find our bliss,
Surrendering sweetly to each salt-kissed kiss.

Rolling and tumbling, we welcome the splash,
Laughter erupts with each playful crash.
Life is a wave, let's ride it right,
In this watery world of pure delight.

## Shadows in the Sand

Trails of footprints lead the way,
As shadows dance at the end of day.
We dig for treasures buried below,
Turns out it's just a lost water bottle's show!

Kites soaring high with vibrant hues,
While clumsy falls bring us the blues.
Yet here we chuckle, under the sun,
As laughter echoes, we're all just one.

Half-baked castles, towers so lean,
With moats that pledge to keep it clean.
Yet here they crumble, it's part of the game,
The art of beach days, never the same.

Shadows grow long, the day's reprise,
With ocean's stories softly rise.
In this sandy theater, we take a bow,
Life's a beach, oh, look at us now!

## Fluid Mirrors of Emotion

Bubbles rise in the bath, oh so bright,
Reflection of chaos, laughter takes flight.
Rubber ducks float in a whimsical spree,
Splashing joy, soaked with glee.

Water drips from the faucet, rhythmically sways,
It echoes my thoughts in curious ways.
I sing to the soap, the moon is my friend,
In this bath-time concert, let the giggles blend.

Mirror, mirror on the wall, don't you frown,
Let's have a laugh, we won't drown.
Waves of silliness, sparking delight,
With each bubble bursting, the scene feels just right.

In the whirlpool of feelings, I find my flair,
Dressed in lather, I float on air.
Who knew emotions could wash and play?
In this playful pool, I'm here to stay.

## Dunes of Desire

Grains of sand like thoughts in my head,
Shifting and slipping, I'm easily led.
A castle of dreams, I build way too high,
Only to watch as the waves say goodbye.

Seagulls cackle, they chase my coat,
In the breeze, I feel like a boat.
Finding treasure in pieces of drift,
Each sandy step is a wobbly gift.

Oh, the sun plays tricks on my melon,
With visions of ice cream, and jelly bean felons.
What's that? A mirage? Or is it just me?
Wandering these dunes, wild and free.

Ebbing and flowing, my wants come and go,
Like a beach ball dancing, putting on a show.
In this realm of desire, I laugh and I sigh,
For every wish granted, another wave goes by.

## The Whispering Sea's Lament

The sea whispers secrets, oh so sly,
Tales of fish with dreams that fly.
Octopuses in tuxedos, ready to dance,
Crabs in pink slippers, oh what a chance!

The waves talk back, they chuckle and tease,
While jellyfish float like jelly on cheese.
Seashells giggle, echoing the breeze,
Tickling the toes of beachgoer's knees.

Underneath the surface, a party awaits,
Sea creatures spinning, with magical plates.
Will the whale sing opera? Will the shark do a jig?
In this watery realm, I leap and I dig.

The ocean's a comedian, making me grin,
With all of its quirks, how could I not win?
So, here in the shimmer under a bright moon,
I join the sea's laughter, a joyful tune.

## Celestial Currents

Stars like fish in a cosmic soup,
Swimming through space in a glittery loop.
I float on my dreams like a cosmic kite,
Chasing the comets, oh what a sight!

Galaxies twist in hilarious ways,
Planets with parties that last for days.
Mars wears a hat, Venus brings snacks,
Uranus in polka-dots, and laughter it cracks.

Asteroids bop to a disco beat,
While Saturn brings rings for a dance-off sweet.
Gravity's goofy, I twirl and I gleam,
In this cosmic ballet, I'm living the dream.

From nebulae clouds to the moon's bright grace,
I whirl with the stars in a happy embrace.
With each cosmic chuckle echoing wide,
I ride the sweet waves of the universe's tide.

## The Song of Salt and Sand

The beach is calling, come on, let's dance,
With grains of sand caught in our pants.
The waves keep laughing, what a funny sound,
While seagulls steal fries, they fly all around.

We build our castles, they crumble and splat,
With moats of water, oh, isn't that fat?
We splash like dolphins, our joy on display,
Until someone yells, 'Hey! Watch out, my way!'

The tide plays tricks, it pulls and it tugs,
We just want sun, but we get all the bugs.
We chase the retreat, it chuckles with glee,
What a silly day at the beach, don't you agree?

Our picnic's a mess, crumbs cling to our face,
We giggle and munch in this salty embrace.
The sun dips low, and we wave goodbye,
To the cheeky waves that wink and sigh.

## Windswept Whispers

The wind it howls, a troublesome friend,
It snatches my hat, will it ever end?
I run like the wind, but I laugh at the chase,
What a wild journey in this airy space.

The dunes are my playground, so soft and so bright,
I tumble and giggle, what a silly sight!
Each grain of sand sticks to my ice cream cone,
A crunchy surprise that I didn't want known.

Seagulls are squawking, they plot and they scheme,
They dive for my snack, in a feathered dream.
I defend my chips with a fierce little battle,
As they whirl around like a feathery cattle.

With each gust of laughter, we take to the sea,
In a splash of mischief, just my friends and me.
Windswept whispers wrap us in delight,
What a joy it is, to take flight tonight.

## Fiesta of Ebbing Bliss

The tide rolls in for a party tonight,
With buckets and shovels, our spirits take flight.
We dance on the shore, with foam on our toes,
Like mermaids we giggle as the water flows.

Surfboards are bobbing, they twist and they spin,
And I trip on a wave, now that's where I've been!
With laughter behind me and seaweed ahead,
I high-five a crab on the sandy spread.

The sun sets slowly, it blushes and beams,
While sandcastles fall like our wildest dreams.
We toast with our drinks, umbrellas in sight,
In this fiesta of joy, everything feels right.

As darkness envelops our silly charade,
We sing to the sea, let our fears fade.
With each crashing wave, a chuckle ignites,
In this ebbing bliss, our happiness unites.

## The Ocean's Invitation

Oh, dear ocean, you toss and you turn,
With bubbly invitations, how do we learn?
You splash and you swirl, a mischievous tease,
Underneath your surface, what secrets are these?

With a wink and a giggle, you beckon us near,
To surf on your waves, without any fear.
But one little slip, and whoosh—down we go,
Like jellyfish dancing in a salty show.

Your treasures are hidden in the depths so vast,
With fish that wear hats, they swim very fast.
We wave to the dolphins, they leap and rejoice,
With each splash of water, we find our own voice.

So here we come back, to enjoy what you bring,
In your playful embrace, we laugh and we sing.
Oh, sweet blue wonder, with your glowing allure,
How joyful it feels, in your depths, we're secure.

## Dancing with the Seafoam

When seafoam tickles toes at dawn,
I laugh and twirl, dancing on.
With a splash and giggle, I take my chance,
The ocean waves, they join my prance.

Seagulls squawk, but I know the beat,
They're jealous of my saltwater feet.
As seaweed wigs sway left and right,
We're the best dancers under the sunlight.

Crabs snap claws, think they can compete,
But no one moves like I do on the fleet.
Shells clink like maracas, a sandy band,
We shimmy and shake upon the land.

So come join the fun, don't be a bore,
The sea's playful spirit's hard to ignore.
With laughter and bubbles, we'll sing a tune,
Dancing with seafoam beneath the moon.

## Descent into the Briny Depths

I took a dive, my head went down,
Into the briny, it starts to drown.
Where fish wear suits and dolphins debate,
On whether seaweed's a culinary fate.

A jellyfish floats, a party balloon,
Saying, "Dance with me, it's always a boon!"
But knock over coral, you'll ruin the fun,
And watch the sea cucumbers run from the sun.

An octopus juggling, oh, what a sight,
His ink splatters like a confetti fight.
I slipped on a clam, went tumbling fast,
With sea urchins laughing, I knew I was last.

The depths may be dark, but smiles spread wide,
In the briny abyss, it's a wacky ride.
So hold your breath and join in the jest,
For laughter below is simply the best!

## The Longing of the Deep Blue

Oh deep blue, I want to dive and play,
But the fish are having a swim meet today.
They'll call me a landlubber, that would just sting,
As I wade and splash, like a fool on a swing.

A flip flop flung, a beach ball above,
They laugh at my "safety" from the ocean's glove.
But with every wave that crashes on me,
I hear the fish laugh, all wild and free.

They challenge my courage with a bubble war,
Sending swirls and giggles, I can't take it anymore!
So I'll cannonball in, make a splashy debut,
And show them that land-lovers can swim like a blue.

But as I charge forth, what a sight to behold,
For I'm more of a splash than a brave, daring gold.
Yet laughter is born from this slippery bound,
An anthem of joy in the sea's sonorous sound.

## A Journey through Nautical Shadows

In shadows of ships, where sailors once roamed,
I trip over barnacles, thinking I've flown.
Whispers of mermaids echo and tease,
As I tumble through mystic brine with ease.

A lighthouse laughs, flickering its light,
"Watch your step, you might lose your sight!"
But I tackle the waves like a pro on a quest,
While krakens ponder, "Who's this silly guest?"

Pirate ghosts chuckle over their grog,
As I fumble to dance with an old eerie fog.
With a map made of jelly, I'm lost, oh dear,
But laughter prevails as the end draws near.

So here's to the shadows, the giggles, the lore,
Where nautical pathways open new doors.
A journey worth taking, with friends by my side,
In the depths of the ocean, where silliness hides.

**Falling Leaves on the Ocean's Breath**

Leaves dance on waves like they've got the groove,
Fishes laugh as they make their moves.
Seagulls swoop down for a popcorn treat,
Nature's snack time is hard to beat.

Drifting debris with hats made of foam,
Crabs in tuxedos, far from their home.
Salty snacks swim, they're quite the thrill,
Underwater chuckles, can you hear the shrill?

Beach balls bouncing 'neath the sunny glare,
Jellyfish twirl like they just don't care.
With a splash and a giggle, pierce the blue,
The ocean's a circus, just for you!

So take off your shoes, come wiggle your toes,
Join the sea creatures in their splashy prose.
From drifting leaves to the waves' funny games,
Life's a big party, and all are fair game!

## Constellations of the Deep

Stars twinkle under the ocean's façade,
Fish play hide and seek, oh my, how bizarre!
Octopi juggle pearls with a wink and a nudge,
Their laughter bubbles up, just can't hold a grudge.

Squid ride glow-in-the-dark waves with flair,
Starfish compete for the best fashion wear.
Anemones dance like they're on Broadway,
With bright neon colors, they brighten the play.

Eels in tuxedos shimmy with grace,
While turtles throw parties, a shell of a place.
A conch shells the gossip, spreading tales,
Of mermaids sneaking snacks from wayward sails.

So let's dive deep to the whimsical night,
Where all creatures glitter in the soft moonlight.
Underwater giggles and shimmery bling,
In the cosmos of sea, let the laughter ring!

## Rhythm of Wandering Souls

Ghostly giggles drift on a wind's embrace,
Lost socks whisper tales of their funny chase.
Mischief bubbles up from a ghoulish seam,
As they tango with shadows in a quirky dream.

Casper just spilled juice, it stains his sheet,
While ghouls take a break for a midday treat.
With popcorn in hand, they cha-cha around,
In a spectral fiesta that knows no bounds.

Zombie's forgotten what it means to moan,
Spinning in circles, they dance like they're stoned.
Even goblins snicker, with their pointy hats,
In a goofy parade, oh imagine that!

So join the parade with your most playful grin,
For every lost soul has a dance to begin.
In the rhythm of laughter, our spirits awake,
In a world full of giggles, let's shimmy and shake!

## Beneath the Surface

Down below, where fish all swim,
I ponder life, it gets quite grim!
The little crabs, they scuttle round,
Avoiding thoughts, they can't be found.

A seaweed hat atop my head,
Makes me look like I'm half-dead!
I wave to dolphins, they just laugh,
My thoughts, it seems, are not enough.

Bubble thoughts up to the sky,
Hoping mermaids will drift by.
With jest and giggles, they swim near,
And turn my frown into a cheer.

So here I'll stay, below the foam,
Where silliness feels just like home!
Each thought a fish, they flip and dive,
In this weird world, I feel alive.

## The Celestial Sea

Stars above, they twinkle bright,
I wonder if they're out of sight.
Squidlike aliens swim around,
In this space, what fun I found!

With jellyfish that glow and wink,
They share their cosmic thoughts to think.
They giggle in their squishy way,
And pull me in their dance and sway.

Cosmic waves, they tickle my mind,
In this odd place, I'm unconfined.
With stars for friends, I lose my cares,
As laughter floats upon the airs.

So sail I will through this bright sea,
A silly trip, just her and me!
In cosmic depths, we splash and twirl,
With giggles echoing, we swirl.

## Isle of Introspection

On an isle made of sandy dreams,
I collect shells and giggle at beams.
Thoughts tumble like waves on the shore,
Each one a treasure I can't ignore.

Crabs play poker in the sun's glow,
While I ponder the meaning of dough.
Do cookies feel guilt when they crumble?
In this funny place, I laugh and tumble.

Banana peels lie all around,
A slip of fate lurks on this ground.
As I muse on life's little quirks,
The trees respond with silly jerks.

So let me lounge on this comical isle,
Where deep thoughts and laughter reconcile.
In introspection, I've found my role,
Swaying gently, tickling the soul.

## **Mermaids of the Mind**

Mermaids dance in my head at night,
Twisting thoughts, it's quite a sight!
One sings loudly, steals my pen,
While bubbles chatter now and then.

They speak of hairstyles, wild and free,
With seaweed braids, just wait and see!
A little dolphin rolls on through,
He brings my cereal, quite the view!

With each thought, a splash, a dive,
In this mind, I feel alive!
They tickle me till laughter flows,
As the silliness just grows and grows.

So here I float, a giggling fool,
In a sea where dreams take the rule.
Mermaids grant wishes with a wink,
In the ocean of thought, who needs to think?

## Navigating the Unknown

In the wild sea of thought, I float,
A rubber duck on a life-sized boat.
Directions unclear, waves that tease,
I follow the gulls; they do as they please.

I asked a fish for some clever tips,
He just winked and flipped his fins and quips.
A crab offered me a map of sand,
But it led to nowhere, it was quite unplanned.

With seagulls squawking, I check my phone,
Why is the ocean always on loan?
I fish for answers in a soda can,
And find that life's just a big prank plan.

So here I am, on this quirky quest,
Paddling through giggles, I'm feeling blessed.
With sharks in tuxedos, life feels absurd,
This sailing business is quite the word.

## Horizon of Hope

As the sun dips down, turn on the light,
I spot a jellyfish wearing a bowtie.
Who knew the horizon could look so chic?
I'll sip my punch—no need to be meek.

Clams throw a party, come join the dance,
With dance moves that make you take a chance.
The waves break laughter, a bubbly sound,
Joy's secret is found where silliness abound.

Now a dolphin sports shades, so dapper and fine,
They surf through the waves, sipping some brine.
While I, on the sand, with sunscreen I daub,
Contemplate if I'm the whale or the blob.

A lighthouse cheers me, its beam so bright,
It sparkles with jokes like stars in the night.
So here's to the laughter, the glimmer of hope,
In this wild ocean, we learn how to cope.

## **Fluid Realms of Thought**

In waters of wisdom, my mind goes afloat,
I paddled in circles—what's that in my coat?
A fish with a monocle, oh dear, oh my,
Said he'd teach me to swim, but he ran off to fly.

The jellybeans ocean is sweet and so wild,
With flavors from dreams that can't be reviled.
I surf on ideas like they're candy waves,
Finding joy in the quirks that each thought behaves.

Thoughts bubble and fizz, a soda pop spree,
Each moment's a giggle, come float here with me!
There's a dolphin accounting my wink and my grin,
Says, "Catch the next wave, let the fun times begin!"

In the pool of my mind, let's dive, take the leap,
With each splash of madness, our laughter runs deep.
In fluidity's grip, let's break the control,
For life's just a swim in the ocean of soul.

## Sailing Through Shadows

Through shadows I sail, on a boat made of bread,
With a crew made of squirrels, ideas in my head.
They chatter and chatter, and point to the stars,
While I steer the ship past candy bars.

The moon waves hello, with a wink in his eye,
He's got a collection of wishes awry.
A shadow of doubt tried to hitch a free ride,
But I launched a coconut; he quickly complied.

With cheese for a sail, and nuts for the oars,
We navigate giggles and mythical shores.
The sea winds whisper secrets in code,
As I dodge the jellyfish, each wearing a robe.

So here's to the shadows that dance in the night,
With laughter as fuel, and dreams in our sight.
For sailing through darkness can be quite the thrill,
Where humor is compass, and joy is the will.

## Secrets of the Salty Breeze

The ocean whispers goofy tunes,
As seagulls dance on salty spoons.
Shells giggle, hiding from the sand,
While barnacles boogie, quite unplanned.

Waves tickle toes and splash the shore,
Crabs wear hats, oh, such a score!
Jellyfish jive with a squishy flair,
And dolphins toast to salty air.

Fish flip flop, their scales a-glint,
While seaweed sways with a wiggly hint.
A clam sings high, a shrimp beats low,
In this salty circus, watch the show!

Bubbles bubble with silly glee,
Each splash bringing waves of jubilee.
The secrets here are silly and grand,
In the salty breeze, life's just unplanned.

## Crashing Heartbeats

The waves collide with a hello,
Crashing rhythms in a buoyant flow.
Shells start a beat, the sea's pop band,
While starfish tap dance on the sand.

A whale cracks jokes with a hearty laugh,
While crabs form lines for a funny autograph.
Seashells giggle, a chorus so sweet,
As fish waltz by on their finned feat.

In this ocean's mix, laughter reigns,
Octopus tickles with playful gains.
The tides play tricks, a funny game,
As sea cucumbers join in the fame.

Heartbeats crash like waves at play,
In this salty haven, we joke away.
With frothy laughs, as bright as sun,
Life's a jest, and oh, what fun!

## **Lost in Liquid Dreams**

In the depths where wild fish flip,
A mermaid calls for a water trip.
Octopi juggle, each tentacle proud,
While turtles snooze, forming a cloud.

Swirling wonders, a whimsical dance,
Plankton winks as they catch a glance.
Corals giggle in shades so bright,
Playing hide and seek well into night.

Drifting off in a soggy state,
Seashells tell tales of a dinner date.
With a splash! A dolphin takes a dive,
In liquid dreams, we all come alive.

Giggling waves and bubbles that pop,
Ride the currents, but don't ever stop.
Lost in laughter, where wishes gleam,
Together we swim in a wavy dream.

## Flowing Memories

Waves whisper stories, sweet and weird,
Of crabs that dance and fish that cheered.
The moonlight giggles on rippling streams,
Sharing secrets like silly dreams.

Ocean breezes bring ticklish tales,
Of starfish sailing with less-than-great sails.
Jellyfish float with a wobbly grace,
While sea turtles wear a smiling face.

Driftwood holds memories of laughter spread,
As dolphins recall the pranks they've led.
In swirling waters, past dances glow,
As the salty echoes of fun overflow.

Each wave carries a chuckle so bright,
In flowing memories, hearts take flight.
So gather 'round, let the fun begin,
In the ocean's arms, we all fit in.

## The Ocean's Embrace

A jellyfish floats, quite aloof,
It dances like it's on a roof.
A seagull steals my tasty snack,
I chase him down, but he won't go back.

The waves crash in with a sly grin,
They whisper secrets, where to begin?
I trip on sand, my castle's fate,
The ocean laughs—it's a funny trait.

A crab in a suit walks sideways fast,
He's late for work; hope he won't be last!
The starfish cheers him on with pride,
"Just keep on crawling, don't you hide!"

With each splash, my worries float,
Laughing hard, I lose my coat.
The ocean's giggle fills the air,
In its embrace, I shed my care.

## Serenity in the Storm

The rain drops down like a wild show,
Umbrellas flip, oh what a blow!
I'm soaked to the bone, but can't complain,
The ducks are quacking, they love the rain.

Lightning strikes like a slapstick gag,
The thunder rolls—a giant brag!
I spin and twirl, lost in the fun,
Who knew chaos could weigh a ton?

Puddles turn into my dance floor,
Splashing around, I just want more.
A gust of wind pulls me off track,
I land on my back with a loud whack!

Yet through the storm, I wear a smile,
The world's a joke, and joy's the style.
As nature rumbles with grumpy cheer,
I laugh out loud, there's nothing to fear.

## Castaway Thoughts

Stranded on this sandy hill,
With thoughts so wild, my mind won't still.
A coconut rolls past my nose,
I give it a push, "Where do you go?"

I'm making friends with driftwood sticks,
Telling tales of my beach tricks.
I build a fire with seashell might,
But it fizzles out—what a funny sight!

A seagull lands and starts to stare,
"Are you the king?" I call in despair.
He squawks and flaps, all things absurd,
Laughing at my silly words.

Lost in a world of my own design,
With laughter and whims, I think I'm fine.
In this cocoon, oh what a prize,
Living my dreams beneath sunny skies.

## The Shore of Self

On the shore, I gather shells,
Each one's a story that surely tells.
Of pirate dreams and mermaid songs,
Life's a beach where laughter belongs.

I dip my toes in the foamy surf,
Each wave's a giggle, a playful lurf.
I pose like a crab, with claws held high,
Pretending to scold the clouds in the sky.

Time drips like the sea from my hands,
Like running jokes across golden sands.
I wave at the jellyfish doing ballet,
Together we dance, come what may.

With sand in my hair and joy as my guide,
Every moment's an oceanic ride.
In this world, so merry and bright,
I find my bliss, oh what delight!

## Glimmers of Hope Amidst the Swells

The waves went laughing, a cheeky embrace,
As jellyfish danced with a grin on their face.
Crabs in tuxedos, so fancy, so spry,
Tipped their top hats and waved us goodbye.

Seashells were gossiping, secrets they kept,
While starfish argued, their days mis-stepped.
A whale gave a wink, oh such a delight,
As dolphins played tricks in the moon's soft light.

## **Footprints that Fade**

On sandy shorelines, we frolicked with glee,
Leaving our footsteps, as bold as can be.
But the waves giggled, 'How silly they seem,'
And washed them away like a bad, silly dream.

With flip-flops a-flapping, we raced with the tide,
But seagulls stole snacks, oh where could they hide?
Our footprints may vanish, they don't stand a chance,
Yet memories linger, like a fishy romance.

## Beneath the Surface, the Silence Speaks

Bubbles of laughter arise from the deep,
With fish telling tales that will make you leap.
The octopus rolls its eyes in disdain,
As clams keep their secrets with no need for pain.

A quiet surprise in kelp gardens grows,
With sea horses giggling at everyone's woes.
They whisper of wonders in colors so bright,
While the seaweed parties all through the night.

## The Serenade of Aquatic Dreams

In dreams of the ocean, the music swells,
With coral choirs casting melodic spells.
A fish in a bow tie conducts the show,
While shrimp play the tambourine, oh what a glow!

The seashells all chime in, a hilarious tune,
And turtles do polkas beneath the bright moon.
What joy in the surf, in the splash and the spray,
As laughter and melody dance through the spray.

# **Echoes of the Past on Water's Edge**

Waves crashed softly on my feet,
Memories danced, oh what a treat!
Fish can't remember where they've been,
I laugh at all the trouble seen.

Seagulls squawk their ancient tales,
Of treasure hunts and windy gales.
Every shell contains a jest,
Nature's humor at its best.

Sandcastles crumble, oh what a sight,
Just like my jeans after one night.
Histories washed out to the sea,
A relay race of folly, whee!

No need to be solemn or grave,
The ocean's a fixer of every wave.
So I build again, with whimsy and cheer,
Echoes of the past, we have nothing to fear.

## The Floating Thoughts of Solitude

In my boat, I float all day,
With thoughts that drift and sway.
A fish whispers, 'What's the plan?'
I reply, 'Not a clue, my finned friend!'

Clouds drift by like lazy sheep,
While I ponder naps, not deep.
A crab jests, 'Where's your destination?'
I shrug, embracing my vacation.

Seaweed questions my choices bold,
'Is it freedom or just old?'
I laugh aloud and wave goodbye,
To worries that went sailing by.

The sun dips low, a golden grin,
My floating thoughts begin to spin.
With every splash, I set them free,
In solitude, I find my glee.

## A Seafarer's Soliloquy

Oh salty breeze, you tease me so,
Swapping stories only you know.
The compass spins, yet here I stand,
With a sandwich in my trembling hand.

The ocean's vast, it sways and hums,
While I wonder where all the fun comes.
Seashells giggle, they know the score,
As I trip on the deck—what a bore!

Fish flip-flop, doing acrobat tricks,
While I fumble more than a box of bricks.
Yelling at waves, 'What's the deal?'
They chuckle back, 'Time to get real!'

Yet, every fall brings joy in disguise,
With laughter echoing through the skies.
So I raise my mug—cheers to the sea,
For every blunder sets my spirit free.

## Chasing the Gentle Undercurrent

Paddling along, I seek my fate,
In waters calm, but oh, I wait.
A turtle shouts, 'You're going slow!'
'No rush!' I retort, enjoying the flow.

Bubbles rise like thoughts in my head,
Who needs to worry when I'm well-fed?
The fish sidestep a dance, quite rare,
While I try to twirl with salty hair.

Seashells laugh, they must have seen,
The attempts I make, so quite routine.
With playful waves, they splash and swirl,
In this grand adventure, I'm just a girl.

Chasing the whispers the currents share,
Finding humor in ocean air.
Each ripple tells a tale to be told,
As I dance and giggle, forever bold.

## The Rhythm of Desire

In a dance with chocolate cake,
I twirl and spin, make no mistake.
Ice cream whispers sweet delight,
While I prepare for an appetite fight.

Banana peels on kitchen floors,
My heart races as the fridge door soars.
With every bite, I slide and glide,
In this scrumptious joy, I take great pride.

Lemonade spilling in the sun,
Sipping joy, oh, it's such fun!
Yet my straw seems to take a swim,
A hilarious chase on a whim.

Chasing snacks like a cheerful fool,
Life's a carnival, oh so cool!
When cravings strike, it's quite absurd,
But laughter's the best flavor, I've heard!

## Undercurrents of Emotion

My cat stares at the wall so keen,
Plotting mischief, like a scene.
Funny how she leaps and bounds,
In her world, with secret sounds.

The mailman arrives, a comic face,
She pounces like she's in a race.
Behind curtains, her antics display,
While I giggle at her ballet.

Feeling lost in a sock drawer mess,
Finding mismatches, a game to assess.
Each hidden treasure brings a grin,
As I jump in with great chagrin.

Like washing socks that vanish at sea,
Left is the mystery, where could they be?
With every sock, a chuckle and sigh,
Finding humor makes time fly!

## **Fleet of Foot**

Running late but full of cheer,
Tripping over my shoes, oh dear!
I zoom past ducks, honking away,
As they quack, I dance in dismay.

With sneakers squeaking on the ground,
I stumble, but laughter's what I found.
A sprightly jog turns into a show,
As I wave to the folks moving slow.

My neighbor waves, I miss the cue,
Instead, I trip right by their view.
Rolling like a tumbleweed, I fly,
Giggles erupt, as I wave goodbye!

Speedy moves, I perfected my art,
But grace? That's not really my part.
In this clumsy act, I am bold,
Life's a comedy, waiting to unfold!

## **Drift of Heart**

Floating dreams on a paper boat,
Sailing wishes while I gloat.
My thoughts like jelly on a spoon,
Wobble gently, oh so soon.

Love's a dance, a silly jig,
With socks as partners, oh so big!
Twisting and laughing through the night,
In this joyous, heart-filled flight.

A kite soars high, tangled and free,
Chasing clouds, just like me.
With every gust, I fall and rise,
Finding giggles in the skies.

The heart drifts on, with playful flair,
Kite strings tugging at the air.
Each smile's a reminder, a gentle tease,
In this voyage, the spirit's at ease!

**Salty Dreams**

Upon the shore, the waves convene,
With buckets and shovels, we set the scene.
Building castles strong and grand,
Until the tide flips through like a band.

Salty snacks, I munch with glee,
As seagulls swoop and steal from me!
With a crunch, laughter spills all around,
My snack attack suddenly unwound.

Tidal pools full of wiggly friends,
A curious crab, my giggle sends.
With silly embraces, we splash and play,
In salty fantasies that won't fade away.

As sun sets low, the skies in hues,
I dream of dolphins and sandy shoes.
With each wave, my heart finds bliss,
In funny moments, I can't resist!

## **Aquatic Reveries**

Fish wear tiny hats, quite dapper,
Swimming with a flair, oh what a caper!
Crabs play cards on the sandy floor,
Laughing as they shuffle, always wanting more.

Seashells gossip, spinning tales so grand,
Whispers of the ocean, all perfectly planned.
Starfish dance like they're in a new wave,
While dolphins dive and the seabed they crave.

Bubbles float up, they tickle my toes,
Making me giggle as everyone knows.
Mermaids sing songs from days gone by,
Giggling at sailors who think they can fly.

A treasure chest filled with jokes and fun,
Pirates chuckle as they dance in the sun.
The waves crash lightly, a soft serenade,
As I splash along, never feeling delayed.

## **Beneath the Moonlit Waves**

Under the moon, the jellyfish glow,
Waving their tentacles, putting on a show.
Octopuses juggle with marvelous ease,
While turtles spin stories of oceanic frisbees.

Crickets in the sea, they chirp and they strum,
Creating a band that makes everyone hum.
The starfish croon, making water hearts swell,
While sea cucumbers giggle and yell.

Seahorses trot in a comical march,
Leading the parade under starlight's arch.
Mussels chuckle at every small wave,
Claiming they're too cool to ever behave.

When morning breaks, they'll all say goodbye,
With laughter so loud, it reaches the sky.
So here's to the night and its magical spin,
The ocean's a party, let the laughter begin!

## **Ripples of Memory**

Each ripple reminds me of flips and of flops,
Seagulls with ice cream, oh how the fun never stops!
Nautical knickknacks in a rush to delight,
Dancing like characters, oh what a sight!

Forgotten sea treasures, a shoe, and a hat,
Singing sweet ballads, a tune just like that.
The old pirate ghost is serenading the bay,
With a wiggle and jiggle, he sways all day.

Barnacles grumble about life and the tide,
Cranky old oysters trying to hide.
The clams all burst laughing, it's quite the affair,
As they open wide with their stories to share.

With every wave's rush, a chuckle they send,
Those memories echo, and laughter won't end.
So here's to the ocean, its quirks and its quirks,
A world that's so funny, where laughter works!

## The Call of the Current

Oh, the current is calling, with a playful shout,
As fishes swim by, flapping all about.
Crab races commence, a nail-biting scene,
With the winner serving up seaweed cuisine.

The seaweed does wiggle, it dances with glee,
While a clam plays it cool, sipping brine with tea.
Seashells, they chant, "We're here for a beach day!"
Fancy flippers in tow, come join the array!

The whirlpools do giggle, they twirl with grace,
While tides make faces, such a silly place!
Dolphins make jokes as they flip in the spray,
It's all in good fun, come laugh and stay!

So heed the water's beckoning cheer,
For under the waves, it's laughter we hear.
With a splash and a laugh, let the currents invite,
Join the watery antics, oh what a delight!

## The Rhythm of the Deep

In the ocean where fish play,
Seaweed dances, hip-hip-hooray!
Crabs practice their ballet prance,
While jellyfish float in a goofy trance.

Waves are like laughter, bubbly and bright,
Seagulls squawk jokes, taking flight.
"Why did the fish blush?" they all chime,
"Because it saw the ocean bottom shine!"

A dolphin dives with a splashy cheer,
Saying, "Let's party, the coast is clear!"
Octopuses spin in a colorful show,
Wearing their hats, what a sight to behold!

So come join the splash, make a big scene,
With fins and laughs, you know what I mean.
When the waves roll in, they teach us to smile,
In the rhythm of the deep, let's dance for a while.

## Murmurs from the Abyss

Deep down where the funny things dwell,
A fish tells tales, oh, can you tell?
With a wink and a grin, it starts its spiel,
About a mermaid with a bubblegum meal.

Starfish gossip with crabs on the floor,
"Did you hear? It rained donuts galore!"
They giggle and wiggle, losing their wits,
In the depths of the ocean, everyone fits.

Eels wrap in jokes, all slippery and sly,
"I'm a snake in the water, oh my, oh my!"
They whisper and chuckle in glimmering night,
Such silly creations, a humorous sight!

So listen closely when you take the plunge,
In the bends of the blue, there's laughter to lunge.
Murmurs from below will tickle your toes,
In the giggly depths, the fun just flows.

## **Boundless Waters of Yearning**

In the sways of the sea, where dreams take a ride,
Fish zoom by, shouting, "Join us, don't hide!"
"Life is a splash, so have some fun,
We'll play leapfrog until we're done!"

A whale sings low, a tune so absurd,
Says, "I lost my hat; it's flying with birds!"
The waves giggle in harmony with glee,
As creatures emerge for a comedy spree.

Bright colors whirl in a vibrant ballet,
Squid twirl and spin, what a humorous fray!
"Catch me if you can!" floats a silly fish,
Their laughter echoing like a big, bold wish.

So frolic and flip in this boundless spree,
For in waters of yearning, all are carefree.
With every splash, let your worries depart,
Join the party of waves, it'll lighten your heart.

## The Calm After the Storm

After the ruckus, the sea starts to grin,
Barnacles chuckle, "Let the fun begin!"
Doves in the sky throw a hush on the flood,
As the sea floor sparkles in glittering mud.

"Why so serious?" a sea turtle remarks,
"Life is a game, let's light up this park!"
With a flip and a flap, the day starts anew,
While krill throw a bash, just for me and you.

The clouds roll away, like a bad ol' joke,
"Guess the shark's a comedian, watch him poke!"
The ocean laughs low, gently swaying along,
In the calm after chaos, the fun dances strong.

So let's celebrate peace, with a splash and a cheer,
Finding humor in troubles, they'll vanish, have no fear.
In the hush of the waves, feel the joy emanate,
For even the wildest storms know how to celebrate.

www.ingramcontent.com/pod-product-compliance
Lightning Source LLC
Chambersburg PA
CBHW060138230426
43661CB00003B/479